HERE
WE
SETTLE

PEMA DÜDDUL

This book first published 2022

Timeless Awareness Publications

www.timelessawareness.org

Second Edition

Australian National Library Cataloguing in Publication Data

A catalogue record for this book is available from the
Australian National Library

Copyright © 2022 Pema Düddul

The poems Simple Awareness, Let Me Let Go and Simply
Awaken were first published in *Resting in Stillness* by Jamyang
Tenphel & Pema Duddul (Jalu Presss, 2020).
All rights for this book reserved. No part of this book may
be reproduced, stored in a retrieval system, or transmitted,
in any form or by any means, electronic, mechanical,
photocopying, recording or otherwise, without the prior
permission of the copyright owner.

ISBN (13): 978-0-6483972-8-1

HERE WE SETTLE

DEDICATION

Dedicated to my heart teacher, Kyabje Dudjom Rinpoche, Jigdral Yeshe Dorje, and to my other teachers: Ngakpa Karma Lhundup Rinpoche, Dungse Namgay Dawa Rimpoche, and Jetsunma Tenzin Palmo.

Homage to the guru!

Dedicated also to my teaching partner and partner in life, Jamyang Tenphel.

CONTENTS

Preface 1

Dawntime Poems 5

About the Author 103

PREFACE

The poems in this collection were written over many years, in many places and settings; sometimes in retreat, sometimes while travelling, sometimes in front of the television. Irrespective of where or when they were written they fall into two categories: short poems and haiku that document *a moment of awareness* arising from meditation, mindfulness or devotion; and pieces of pithy prose that came to me in dreams or after Dharma practice.

The poems and haiku, in documenting a single moment, bring attention to the importance of each small fragment of time, of being in the here and now, in our bodies, rather than in our heads looking backwards into the past or anticipating the future. Every moment is a precious jewel, one that can call us into our true nature, the Buddha Nature.

The slightly longer but still pithy pieces are always inspired by my Buddhist teachers or the Dharma itself. Many of the prose works were jotted down immediately after a dream of my heart lama, Kyabje Dudjom Rinpoche, Jigdral Yeshe Dorje. Sometimes these works show a level of insight or understanding that I did not have at the time. These I see as teaching gifts from my lama, guiding me in my practice. Therefore, I give all credit for the words and the insight they hold, and any benefit they may bring, to him.

For me, dharma practice is primarily simple meditation and devotion. The poems touch on these themes as well as others central to Buddhism: the significance of the present moment, impermanence, compassionate ethics, renunciation and *the true nature of the mind*. I have not consciously set out to explore these themes in a didactic way, which is perhaps why the poems do so somewhat unflinchingly but also, at times, with humour and joy.

Every poem or piece of prose collected here has one thing in common. They were all written at dawn immediately after a meditation or practice session or after awakening from a dream. Sometimes they were scribbled on bits of paper in the half dark while I was still only partially awake. Because of this, I feel that they all have a sense of the dawn moment, a *freshness and directness*. Those moments of freshness and direct experience do not only happen at dawn, of course, but for me dawn has always been a special time, a time of solitude and introspection. I hope the poems embody that for the readers of this book.

It is also my wish that this modest collection provides a poetic complement to the many published works on meditation and mindfulness currently available and, rather than reduce meditation practice to theory, reflects the lived experience of an everyday, modern Buddhist. I am a simple Buddhist devotee, not a great meditator, and certainly not a great scholar of the philosophy of Buddhism, but I am committed and *open-hearted*. These are quite common traits but I think they are essential to Buddhist practice in this age of constant distraction. I would like to think that the poems show something of my commitment and open-heartedness so that it might inspire a similar commitment and *openness* in those who read them who are just entering the path.

I am not alone in believing that poetry has the power to embody the heart of the Buddha Dharma in ways that can't be achieved by other kinds of writing.[1] In the Tibetan tradition the study of poetry is considered essential. Poetry can inspire deep insights and prod us into states of mindful

---

[1] See *The Dharma of Poetry: How Poems Can Deepen Your Spiritual Practice and Open You to Joy* by John Brehm (Wisdom Publications, 2021).

awareness and *recognition* of our natural state. Given this, each poem can be used as a touchstone for daily contemplation. To bring the fruit of these contemplations from the head down to the heart the book finishes with a guided meditation designed to ease the reader into a meditation infused with calm and ease.

Though I practice within the Tibetan tradition, specifically the Dudjom lineage of the Nyingma school, this book and the poems and prose it contains can be appreciated by Buddhists of any tradition and indeed by anyone interested in meditation or in using poetry to support contemplation and reflection.

May these poems bring those who read them some benefit, or at least a little enjoyment, and may all beings be well and content.

DAWNTIME POEMS
FROM THE HEART

AH!
Here we all settle
In perfect vivid nowness –
The ultimate teacher;
Which is simply our pure and natural awareness
Just as it is.

Like a stream sparkling under the sun
Flowing always in the one direction
Over all the mossy stones
Through the shallows
And over deeper, darker pools
We too
Steadfastly make our way
To becoming the light

Be at home in yourself
Rest in joyful ease in your natural condition
Everything is okay as it is
Your nature is perfect as it is
Your own fundamental, naked awareness
Is Dzogpachenpo itself —
The wisdom of Samantabhadri

Be at home in yourself
Rest in joyful ease in your natural condition
Everything is okay as it is
Your nature is perfect as it is
Your own mind and its activity
Is Dzogpachenpo itself —
The compassion of Samantabhadra

Be at home in yourself
Rest in joyful ease in your natural condition
Everything is okay as it is
Your nature is perfect as it is
Stop seeking for something elsewhere
Stop wanting to be more than you are
Abandon all your wandering and distractions
And just stay home —
Contented and at ease

Such gentle ease and joy arises
when I remember your face,
my precious lama;
my true heart dawning,
like a full moon rising in a daytime sky.

The chains of the past
And the snares of the future
Are freed in the now.

Take a break
Each day
From the hectic burden of worldly life
To be still and quiet
Until in some ordinary moment
All of a sudden and unexpectedly
You awaken to the delightful truth –
That the universe is permeated with love
A love like a pervasive presence
And that you are that loving presence too

The sun rises in a blush of pink and orange
Wrens twitter playfully in the azaleas

The air frisky on my skin;
Pinking my cheeks to mirror the sky

This moment is happening now, just this once
Precious and unique
Never to be repeated

My heart so, so light with the wonder of it all

POEM FROM THE PREFACE

A moment of awareness
The true nature of the mind
Freshness and directness
Open-hearted, openness
Ah! Recognition

In this present moment:
Release worry and anger and rest in the true nature of all.
Express the natural kindness, openness and honesty that is the manifestation of that true nature.
Give rise to joyous gratitude for the preciousness of life, and share that joy with all.

On my morning perambulations
My cosy walking meditation
I sometimes remember
That the old Mississippi River
Moving at the pace of three miles per hour
(An unhurried stroll)
Is slowly walking home
Just like me

My tender heart song
and the beat of your breathing
are one and the same

Imagine we are all in a rudderless boat
Drifting on a luminous river sparkling with dappled sunlight
Unbothered by the darting of silver-scaled fish
Or the high cry of a heron
Echoing in an otherwise quiet place
Just letting the current carry us along
Slowly, dreamily
No destination, no goal
At ease
Because we know that the current is joy
We know that the current is evenness and love

SIMPLY AWAKEN

We don't need to strive in order to hear, we just hear.
We don't need to strive in order to see, we just see.
We don't need to strive in order to taste, we just taste.
We don't need to strive in order to feel, we just feel.
We don't need to strive in order to smell, we just smell.
We do not need to strive in order to wake,
We simply awaken.

When we stay in the awareness of the moment.
Not classifying, describing or judging what we sense,
Just remaining gently present,
Then we are truly aware, truly awake.

Bright morning light falls
on the form of the Buddha;
the sun's devotion.

I am a misty beech wood in ancient Spain
I am a leaf falling ever so slowly like a yellow feather in a quiet empty garden in sacred Kyoto
I am the universe-echo that is the quiet song of a pearly sea shell on a stretch of wild coast at long, lonely Big Sur
I am a defiant dandelion in long grass by a well-worn footpath in every small town of this strange cosy world
I am a charming Southern oak wearing jazzy ornaments of Spanish moss at blue moon midnight on Bull Street in Savannah Georgia
I am the clip clop of a drag queen's high heels on Saint Anne Street in the French Quarter of New Orleans
I am the heat beating down insistently on salt bush scrub in the boundless and silent red Outback
I am the clapping of hands and stamping of feet on a wooden floor in an old timber church on the edge of a heat-struck town in Mississippi
I am a cherry tree in an orchard in Gifu long bereft of its pink blossoms but rich with fruit, swelling and ripe and sticky to the touch
Most of all I am the joyous laugh of a delighted child
The soft tears of a new widow
The musical sighs of a person's very first love
And, of course, you are all this too

The turbulent waves
Of attachment and aversion,
All our worldly wants and fears,
Break on the shore of our true nature

Sun-shower rainbows,
mossy birdbath in long grass;
we find the same joy.

LET ME LET GO

For those who beat me
Let me have the highest hopes.

For those who steal from me
Let me have endless generosity.

Let me be a friend to those who hate me
And a comfort for all who do me wrong.

Let me not think of some as friend and some as foe
Let me welcome all.

Let me be a good heart
A generous mind.

May I not be afraid to have a broken heart
To see to the pain of the world.

For all those who ultimately are my own,
Let me be free to love.

SITTING

We sit together
On our boogie board meditation mats
Surfing prayer waves
Floating pom-pom cloud-like
On the vast sea-sky of the ocean of wisdom

We drift
Gazing at the cosmos above
As we peer into the expanse within

We have yet to plumb the depths
Though even here on the silver surface
Amongst the ripples of common insight
We sense the clear happy deep awaiting us.

Autumn oak leaves
As red as drops of blood
Scatter all over the sharp grass;
Impermanence is beautifully real.

Under my ribcage
a wild cicada night song;
my joy calling yours.

You said 'My nights are full of exhausting dreams,
my mind is like a mad magician.'
I said 'Awakening completely stops the show.'
Then we smiled from our bones out.

Shivering in a bitter wind
All sense of past and future gone
Time itself carried away by the cold
Leaving us suddenly in the naked now
Naked awareness burning away everything
Cold, hot, me, you
Everything except the raw, tingling energy of life

DO NOT WORRY

Child of Awareness
Do not worry
Those who love and protect you,
The Awakened ones,
Are always near.

Do not worry
Everything you experience
In this brief interval between birth and death
Is a mere fabrication of the deluded mind,
An illusion;
Beyond which is the luminous truth
Of unhindered wellbeing and joy.

Do not worry
Everything you experience
In the interval between falling asleep and waking
Is just a fabrication of the deluded mind,
A dream;
Beyond which is the luminous truth
Of boundless love and compassion.

Do not worry
Everything you will experience
In the interval between death and rebirth
Is only a fabrication of the deluded mind,
A projection;
Beyond which is the luminous truth
Of perfect wisdom and evenness.

Child of Awareness
In the interval
Embrace the luminous truth as it dawns
Or go to the brightest light
And do not worry;
For in that luminous truth is the final awakening,
And in the brightest light is freedom from pain and strife.

Dawn mist crowns the trees,
the light softly luminous;
a joyful heartache.

Morning breeze stirring
the scent of wattle flowers;
skin all a-tingle.

Go for solitude in the forest grove of your own mind.
Rest there in the shade of the true Bodhi tree;
And through that solitude and rest,
Become an everlasting comfort for all the world.

All that you love
> In truth you do not really love

Every feeling you've ever had
> Is nothing more than a fabrication

The things you believe
> In the end you do not truly believe

Whoever you think you are
> You are mistaken

Whatever you think you know about yourself
> Is ultimately false

You are not at all who you think you are
> What you call your "self" is not even here!

And yet, you are so incomprehensibly vast.

Turn inwards to find
your fundamental goodness;
and there finally settle down.

Rain thrums on the roof,
lightning flares at the window;
a dawn thunderstorm.

A soap bubble floating in the air;
the space within fleetingly separated
from the vastness without.
This is what we call the self,
just that sense of separation.
Momentary, delicate, beautiful, yes,
but nothing compared to the boundless luminosity
of the sun-filled sky.
Rejoice then, when the bubble pops,
and the self and the separation are no more.

Pale sliver of moon,
birdcall in the sleepless night;
my lonely heart song.

In love and ease
all comings and goings are effortlessly released,
the turbulent mind at rest at last;
boundless luminous awareness
naturally arisen.

A hidden cascade –
into the cold white tumble
silver-green leaves fall.

When pain strikes
When your body betrays you
Rejoice
The pain is teaching you
That the body is not worth cherishing
Why cherish that which stings you constantly?
Besides, one day your body will perish and rot away

When someone insults you
When you feel slighted and humiliated
Rejoice
The insult is teaching you
The fragility of your ego
And that the self is not worth cherishing
Why cherish that which leads you into emotional traps?
Besides, one day that self will perish
And dissolve into nothing.

When the world disappoints and frustrates you
Rejoice
This is teaching you
That nothing in samsara is worth cherishing
Not a single piece of it is worth anything
Why cherish samsara?
It is a web of deceit and misery that drags you
Into bottomless suffering
Besides, one day every last bit of it will fall apart and perish.

Cherish instead that you have the opportunity to awaken
Cherish your fundamental goodness,
Your unborn and undying natural awareness

Rejoice
In the boundless love and compassion
That is the radiance of that pristine state

Rejoice
That all your pain and suffering is passing
And merely a trigger to turn your mind
Toward that which matters:
Joy, love, compassion and the pristine state of evenness

Sky-like, mind rests clear,
Thoughts dissolve in boundless space;
Awareness abides.

Clouds like bird-shadow
shimmer on a slow river;
we are no more real.

Warm summer morning,
a jealous duck flaps and quacks;
the pond too crowded.

Natural timeless awareness
Is without beginning or end;
A lucid spontaneous presence
That is unwavering, without waxing or waning.

It is the boundless ocean of wisdom;
The very source
From which the waves of appearances and possibilities
Arise
As either samsara or nirvana
Depending on the state of our recognition.

Such a wondrous thing that heaven and hell
Are merely a matter of mind!

Spring indigo skies,
mountain flowers blossoming;
our minds wide open.

Everything we experience or perceive
is a dream-like illusion,
a temporary mirage,
a fleeting fabrication.
Let it all go and rest.

Likewise, thoughts and emotions are dream-like illusions,
mere fleeting fabrications.
Let them go
and let yourself rest.

At the time of dying
all that appears is a dream-like manifestation of mind,
a temporary mirage.
Recognise this and rest.

After everything we held dear has fallen away,
the ultimate luminosity will dawn;
take refuge in that simple clarity
and abide in the infinite rest that is our true nature.

Tall silver ghost gums
bound by tendrils of mist;
stillness and movement.

Smell of summer storms
raindrops singing as they fall;
the earth sighs and steams.

My heart is a hermit

Your own gentle heart its high and quiet mountain refuge

Your bright eyes the vast empty sky that is its cherished solitude and constant grace

Your clear voice its easy pilgrimage to the ancient birthplace of its undying faith

Your soft smile the warm cup of tea it sips on a brittle winter morning that is its only worldly joy

Your tender touch its undistracted bliss in a moment of pure timeless awareness

My heart is a hermit
And you are the sublime reason why

Sitting in winter sunlight
Warm cup of tea in my hands
The hush of a cold morning in my ears
The mind joyfully at ease

Dew on the windows
Clouding the glass
Droplets trickle down
Sparkling with sunlight
Like little rivers of shining diamonds
Delicate, brilliant, luminous
Then gone again when the clouds move in
And even more precious for having only lasted a moment

In our weary minds
thought comes, whirls around, and goes;
like flying embers.

A hushed twilight falls,
a bold swallow courts the moon;
my fingers court yours.

Evening star high and bright
Open fields stretch from horizon to horizon
Light in a distant farmhouse window
A storm bird calls for the coming autumn rains
And I walk the narrow track
Awareness walking with me
Encompassing everything

Here we settle, again
Without contrivance or fabrication
In the mind's basic, natural condition
Just as it is.

Here we settle, again
Undistractedly and with ease
Looking directly at the face of our fundamental nature
Just as it is.

Here we settle, again
Our natural awareness blazing
All cognition liberated without trace upon arising
Just as it is.

Ten million fireflies,
tiny stars in the deep dark;
each a thought of you.

After the hail storm,
damp feathers in the long grass;
a silent sorrow.

To have three hearts is a wondrous thing

I have the heart of my body
        Which is mine but equally yours, my guru

I have the heart of my mind
        Which is yours and only and always yours

And then there is that boundless heart-mind
        That is mine and yours and everyone's
        And no-one's at all

Puddles full of clouds;
a child jumps wildly about
splashing them away.

Sunlight radiance,
clover field on a high hill;
all this just for me?

These thoughts and feelings,
all the play of pure awareness,
all arising and dissolving
within that naked awareness itself
and not separate from it.
To truly see and truly feel the truth of this,
is to break the illusion
of beginning, continuing and ceasing.
And that means no more pointless trouble.

Before you leave me
alone in the dark graveyard
we shiver and kiss.

NO TIME TO WASTE

Focussing on hubris rather than humility
On gratification rather than giving
On cruelty rather than kindness
On affectation rather than true affection
Focussing on form rather than substance
On word rather than meaning
On ritual rather than essence
On elaboration rather than simplicity
On pretending rather than being authentic
Such is a meaningless life.
Abandon everything except the one precious thing:
Recognising the true nature of mind.
There is nothing else to do and no time to waste!

On the meditation cushion
I am like a sole jellyfish
adrift on a vast ocean;
luminous with joy.

Beneath the arbour
a breeze robs my mouth of words;
the wisteria dances.

At the knitting circle
Edith asks 'Is this your first time learning?'
Without looking up from my clumsy needles I say,
'I'm a Buddhist. We don't believe in first times.
No firsts or lasts,
No beginnings or endings,
No arrivals and no departures.
No starts or finishes,
No new or old,
No originals and no copies.
No yesterday, no today and no tomorrow.'
Edith blinks, says,
'Need a cup of tea?'

Morning snowmelt flows
cold on the smooth pebble stones;
a stream of feelings.

Our heart is our true home.

Not the heart of fickle emotions and attachment;
the heart of selfless kindness
and boundless compassion.

Not the heart of me and mine
of holding on
of tightly grasping;
the heart of letting go,
of releasing.

Not the heart of fear and inhibition;
the heart of courageously casting all petty concerns away.

The heart of opening into the limitless space
of giving and caring and love.
That is our true home.

As we awaken
sunlight sparkles on dawn frost;
my heart in your hand.

This broad starry sky;
a magical illusion,
a mirror of mind.

A temple bell rings out
Calling forth the rising sun
Kyoto long awake
Before I yawn and stretch in a tangle of sheets, thinking,
'This place and I are old lovers.'

When your gaze is lost in a light-filled autumn sky
When a gentle breeze goose-pimples your skin
When the scent of wattle and eucalypt
Wakes you to where you are
When you listen joyfully to a wren singing in the garden
When your body thrums with the coming of a storm
Be present with the simple awareness that encompasses all

How marvellous to know that these experiences
Are all the play of mind!

The stillness of snow,
trees like wise black skeletons;
a silent ghost world.

Nose and cheeks quite cold
ears warm under my beanie;
mind so light as sleep comes

SIMPLE AWARENESS

Bathed in rainbow light
Fundamental goodness unfolds
Outer and Inner
No difference
All of the same sweet taste
To Awareness

Simple awareness
- Nothing less than *Rigpa* itself -
Illuminates all
On which it shines its radiance

Nothing beyond it
Nothing hidden from it
Bathed in rainbow light
Everything illuminated
Simple awareness/fundamental goodness
Unfolds

Early winter night;
A crescent moon shines brightly
over the willows.

After the vigil
walking in the dark garden;
moon flowers in bloom.

NEVER LASTING

Like clouds in the sky
All things that exist
All the delights of our five senses
Inevitably dissipate;
never lasting

Like last night's dream
All our endeavours
All our worldly pursuits and efforts
Come to nothing and are already gone;
never lasting

Like autumn frost
Life and love
All that we hold tightly
Will melt away as if under a rising sun;
never lasting

Like wisps of smoke
All our friendships and enmities
All our familial and romantic entanglements
Will simply drift away as if blown by an evening breeze;
never lasting

Never lasting –
Our childhood homes and haunts
So just leave them behind
And go to the wilderness for solitude

Never lasting –
The hardships of the body and struggles of the mind
So there's no point fighting them or fleeing them
Just make them your meditation

Never lasting –
The loneliness and delusion of the imaginary self
So dissolve it completely
By entrusting your heart to joyous devotion

Never lasting –
The misery and pain of mundane existence
So commit your life and heart fully to the Buddha Dharma,
And find there the abiding bliss of your ultimate nature.

In the quiet darkness, calm dawns,
With the clarity of morning light;
A boundless luminosity forever glowing
Like a never-setting sun.

Lying awake in the deep night,
listening to the sound of magnolia blossoms
falling to the dewy ground
with a delicate *phlump*;
such a vast but gentle joy.

On the death of noon
a cloudless sky sings in blue,
echoing my wonder.

My meditating beloved
So persistent and playful
In his boundless devotion
And uninhibited joy

When he smiles I feel so completely happy

IT'S UP TO YOU

Wherever you plant your feet,
May that be the line drawn
Against anger, hatred and violence;
Wherever you stand,
May only compassion, kindness and benevolence abide.

May your presence in the world
Be a bulwark against the tide
Of selfishness, narcissism and greed;
Wherever you are,
May there be selfless concern for others and generosity.

In the face of ignorance, closed-mindedness and egotism,
Show the face of wisdom, open-heartedness and humility.
May you become a light for those in need
And a safe-haven for all.

If it is not you who awakens the power of compassion
The power of selflessness and wisdom
Then who will it be?
It is up to you.
And if not now, then when?

Shady summer days;
My little mind sings out loud
enjoying birdsong.

Like trying to catch a shooting star
        by chasing its reflection on the surface of a lake
Like gazing through a window
        and believing the sky to be square
Like trying to catch a bird
        by casting a net over its shadow
Like gazing at a mirage
        And believing it a cool lake
Like trying to taste an apple
        by reading a description of its sweetness
Like gazing in a dusty mirror
        and thinking our own face is stained

The true nature cannot be grasped
        With the dualistic mind
Best to give up such pointless games
        And simply look to our own awareness
        And rest there in ease and joy

There are a thousand fires
Burning inside all of us;
All the hurts and horrors
Of our endless pasts.
Dousing each of them
One by one
Would take a thousand more years
Than any of us has left to live;
Yet it would take mere moments to extinguish them all
With a heart at one with the Guru.

A lark sings
Frost glistens in the grass
A thin crust of ice turns the half-empty birdbath
Into a cold, imperfect mirror
Glittering like glass with the warming sun;
Reflecting the translucent pink sky of dawn

Frozen just beneath the thin surface
A perfect white magnolia petal;
Like a sunken cloud
Past and future suspended in the ever now

The light always comes
No shadow lasts forever;
Likewise anger, sadness and pain
All fade under the luminous gaze of awareness

The heart dwells on the Buddha
The heart unites with the Buddha
The heart becomes the Buddha
The Buddha *is* the heart
The heart is natural awareness

AWARENESS AND ITS JOYFUL RADIANCE

Nothing external and certainly nothing internal is truly an obstacle to a practitioner. To a true practitioner everything is an ornament of awareness.

The simplest way to recognise this is to soften our attitude toward the things we are labelling obstacles; to adopt an attitude of loving spacious openness to them, neither avoiding them nor holding on to them, simply letting them be as they are.

In a state of relaxed loving openness everything is experienced as the unencumbered and fleeting arising and effortless dissolving of dream-like appearances.

When we practice this total openness in a sustained way we will eventually awaken to the self-perfected natural state, in which everything spontaneously and instantly liberates according to its true nature, which is Shunyata.

In the self-perfected natural state there is no arising and no dissolving. No past, no future and no now. No this and no that. No here, no there and no in-between. No causes and no effects. No form and no formlessness. No subject and no object. No self and no other. No you and no me. There is just natural, lucidly clear awareness and its joyful radiance – boundless love and compassion.

The well of suffering is endless
ever-thirsty, unquenchable
It cannot be sated
        by giving it voice
        or offering it space
        nor by fleeing from it
        or denying it
It is only through love
        and joy
        selfless and boundless
that the poisonous well of the self
finally runs dry

Our natural awareness
Unadorned, naked
Boundless, luminous
Is wisdom perfected
Already overbrimming with blessings
Without anything having been conferred or received
Naturally arisen, naturally abiding
Perfectly complete

Make your heart like the sun and the moon;
Shining freely and openly
On all under the boundless sky.
Day or night, dawn or dusk,
May your light always shine,
Indiscriminately and without limit;
Radiating immeasurable love to each and every being.

In the mountain's breath, rest.
Feel the pulse of being;
Unclouded by thought,
Simply settle as you are.
Grasp at nothing,
Push nothing away;
Let everything be.
Like the flow of a slow river,
Just let it all go.

GUIDED MEDITATION

Make yourself comfortable
Whatever position feels best
Is best

With a spine straight but not tight or taught
Rest your hands on your knees or thighs, palms down;
As a leaf rests on the warm ground

Take a few calming breaths,
Breathing in naturally through the nose
Then a little more slowly out through the mouth
Without effort,
Let your outbreath get a little longer each time

Now,
Go back to breathing naturally
Let your breathing find its own perfect rhythm
And allow yourself to relax

You are safe here
You are safe now
Let all your cares and worries recede into the background;
Like wisps of smoke dissipating on a gentle breeze

Just relax
Just rest

Try not to dwell on the past or anticipate the future
If thoughts come, let them come, but then let them go

Like waves that rise, crest, and sink back into the ocean
Of their own accord
It is in the nature of thoughts and emotions to dissolve
By themselves, without us having to do anything

Just be here, now
Settle into the present moment
Allow yourself to rest; body, speech, mind and heart

Just relax
Just rest

As you gently breathe in
Allow your mind to be infused with calm and tenderness
As you exhale slowly
Allow your body to relax
More and more with every outbreath

With every outbreath
Let go of any tension
With every outbreath
Let all of the muscles in your body relax
From the very top of your skull to the very tips of your toes
Just relax and rest in this present moment;
As a cloud rests in a windless sky

Just relax
Just rest

Now,
Place your awareness on the whole experience of breathing
Very gently
Like a snowflake landing on a lake
Simply be aware
As breath and calm and love flows in,
Simply be aware
As tension, tightness and distraction flows out;

Just rest in awareness, as sunshine rests on the water

If you find yourself distracted
Or swept up in thought
Just gently bring yourself back to awareness
To your breathing
No need to worry
The coming back from distraction is the whole point
Be kind to yourself, and gently return over and over gain

Just relax
Just rest

Simply be here, now
Completely settled in the present moment
Come home to a state of natural rest;
Like a drop of water returning to the vastness of the ocean

Just relax
Just rest

By this effort
May all beings be free of fear, sorrow and pain
May all beings know wellness, tranquillity and love
May all beings abide in the perfect bliss and equanimity
Of their true nature
Om Ah Hung

ABOUT THE AUTHOR

Pema Düddul is a Buddhist Chaplain and the Co-Director of Pristine Awareness: Foundation for Buddhist Practice. Pema has been a Buddhist for forty years, discovering at the age of eleven that his personal worldview and the tenets of Buddhism were in perfect accordance. From the late 1980s he started practising in the Vajrayana, or Tibetan Buddhist, tradition. Pema considers Dudjom Rinpoche, Jigdral Yeshe Dorje (1904-1987) to be his Heart Lama, though they never met in person. Over the years Pema has received teachings from masters in all four schools of Tibetan Buddhism and is completely non-sectarian. In 2005 he received the tantric vows of a ngakpa, the Tibetan Buddhist equivalent of a non-monastic religious minister. He received these vows from one of his principle teachers, Ngakpa Karma Lhundup Rinpoche. Pema has decades of experience as a Buddhist practitioner and has taught mindfulness and meditation in Buddhist, educational and other settings since 2007. Pema is also a certified practitioner of Thought Field Therapy (TFT) and the Emotional Freedom Technique (EFT) or tapping, a therapy very similar to the Tibetan medical practice of Yuk Cho. Pema has both a Masters and a doctorate (PhD) in Creative Writing and is an Adjunct Associate Professor of writing, editing and publishing at the University of New England.

Contact Pema: www.pristine-awareness.org
https://www.facebook.com/PemaDuddul